CATCH
and other poems

Also by Richard Michael Levine

Bad Blood: A Family Murder in Marin County (nonfiction)
The Man Who Gave Away His Organs: Tales of Love
*   and Obsession at Midlife* (fiction)

CATCH

and other poems

Richard Michael Levine

Scarlet Tanager
BOOKS

Cover painting: *Hilly Hardball* by Brianna Mulvale (Gabet)
www.briannasartwork.com

Cover and interior design and composition: Dickie Magidoff

Author photo: Hilary Brodey

Published by Scarlet Tanager Books
P.O. Box 20906
Oakland, CA 94620
www.scarlettanager.com

Library of Congress Cataloging-in-Publication Data

Levine, Richard M.
  [Poems. Selections]
  Catch and other poems / by Richard Michael Levine.
      pages cm
  Includes bibliographical references.
  ISBN 978-0-9768676-4-7 (alk. paper)
  I. Title.
  PS3612.E9265A6 2015
  811'.6--dc23

2014036165

for lovely Lucy

Contents

I

Catch

One of us would say "Let's play catch"
and we'd all grab our oil-treated gloves
and a hardball and go jouncing down
the bumpy hill in the big brown beat-up
Buick with loose suspension
to the town park on Long Island Sound.
The grass was new-mown in rectilinear patterns
or overgrown, feather-soft and dandelion-strewn.
We'd spread out and shout "Liner,"
"Drive me back," "High fly," "Grounder,"
"Send me wide," and Dad would
comply unerringly.
Homer's heroes had nothing
on the Dodgers we imagined being:
fleet-footed Amoros and strong-armed Furillo
or the Duke, prowling center so confidently
he'd make the toughest play seem a snap.
Not us. We'd make the easiest seem hard
to show off all our stuff,
leaping high to snag a fly
a little overhead or diving for a line drive
close by and rolling to a stop.
Even on cloudy days I'd cup my eyes
with both hands waiting for the ball to drop
out of a blinding sun in the nick of time,
then turn to fire home, where Dad would
wince in mock pain to show how much it burned
or pretend to be Campanella tagging out
the winning run sliding to the plate.
Or he'd clap his hands silently
in the distance. What bliss!

It's funny, I don't recall my father
giving me advice about girls and sex
or how to be a man or deal with loss.
All we did was toss a ball.
I don't remember sharing dreams
or secrets with my brother.
Catch was how we talked to one another.

The Good Humor Man

The perfect end of a perfect summer day
Came with beckoning bells from blocks away,
Near the half-hidden sign that read Children At Play.

I was a typical ten-year-old
For whom death was a rumor, sickness a cold,
At the perfect end of a perfect summer day.

I'd run through the humid, cicada-stitched air,
With branches of weeping willows brushing my hair,
Toward the half-hidden sign that read Children At Play,

A dollar flapping in my upraised hand,
Where I was greeted by Jerry, the Good Humor Man,
At the perfect end of a perfect summer day.

He called me Smiley and my brother Red
And always warned us to do as our parents said,
Near the half-hidden sign reading Children At Play.

One evening when he wasn't there I asked,
"Where's Jerry?" to be told, "Son, he's passed."
There were other nearly perfect summer days
But I was no longer among the children at play.

Words

I'll tell you the world's worst word,
Cousin Robert Shear whispers,
if you swear never to say it aloud.
Cross my heart and hope to die,
I answer as he looks around
and breathes into my ear
a harsh, unfamiliar, fearful sound
that might be from the Haggadah
Grandpa, a stoop-shouldered, unsmiling
man who can barely speak English
after more than forty years here,
recites in rapid-fire Hebrew,
bending back and forth,
not caring that we don't understand
or even listen to him but talk about
baseball or the price of things:
houses, new cars, wedding rings.
From my six-year-old point of view
freedom came not from Egypt
but from Brooklyn with a Jewish
exodus to suburban lands where
grass turns green not yellow,
trees aren't wizened or imprisoned
in wire cages at their bases
and some become all red in fall.
On holidays we drive back in serried ranks
of Buicks, Oldsmobiles and Cadillacs
with big tailfins and small windows
like squadrons of invading tanks,
and I learn to read by saying aloud
the signs along the way that sometimes

rhyme or nearly do: Tailor, Shoe Repair,
Hair Salon, U.S. Mail, or if not, are still
beautiful to hear like Stationery Store.
This Passover when Grandpa finishes
and we can finally eat the dry baked
chicken and fried potato latkes
Grandma makes (like hockey pucks,
my dad jokes), then gives out,
based on grades, newly minted silver dollars
she has saved (I always got the most),
I fly, pockets jingling, through
ancient peeling hallways with cracked
black and white floor tiles that reek
of stale cooking grease and pee,
down the street from the public school
to the small wooden shul where
Grandpa spends his life,
shouting as loud as I can:
fuckfuckfuckfuck
fuckfuckfuckfuck....
All ceremony stops, windows open wide
and dumbstruck heads are stuck out,
While I turn back and, breathless, yell
fuck...fuck...fuck...fuck...
fuck...fuck...fuck...fuck...
realizing for the first time that words,
chosen well, can cast a magic spell
that holds the world in its fast grip.

Reading Cereal Boxes

Far better than the sugary flakes
and puffs were the boxes they
came in, with enough fun stuff
on them to last through otherwise
humdrum breakfasts. Who needs
school when you can learn while
eating by reading about famous
sports figures and their stats,
plus recipes, puzzles, contests
(wouldn't Mom be surprised if I won
the Roy Rogers pony) and cartoons
galore featuring Tony the Tiger,
Franken Berry and Count Chocula?
And who needs Hanukkah when
two box tops and a quarter bring
you, say, an Army fort with "injuns"—
these are pre-PC days—riding side-
saddle around it shooting flame-tipped
arrows, or a set of seven cloth-draped
finger puppets with a cardboard TV
screen for them to cavort before,
or baking-soda-powered submarines
and frogmen to put in trays of water?
(I can still feel the thrill of it now.)
Moreover, a cut-out from the box's
back becomes—fold over, tuck in,
fix in place, raise up—a space station
(no matter that it has "taste sensation"
still visible on it), fire engine or
life-sized 3-D picture of Wyatt
Earp's blazing six shooter. And who

needs just another magician pulling
a rabbit from a hat, when crunching
through the cereal brings up,
perhaps, a cellophane-wrapped
"ultrasonic" whistle, "official" Lone
Ranger deputy badge, plastic monkeys
that hang from the bowl, a Superman
belt buckle or Captain Midnight
secret decoder ring, lucky charms
to entwine around your arm or wrist
and countless other equally fine things?

Dr. Mollins' Cabinet of Smiles

Did anyone ever grow up allergy-free and straight-
toothed in the suburbs in those days? Not me,
not my siblings or friends. The weekly shots and
brace tightenings were eased by the neighborhood's
first color TV in Dr. Norwood's waiting room
(once when I asked him what, exactly, was I
allergic to, he said, "Yourself, your own sputum"),
as well as the collection of antique grandfather clocks
fat-fingered, peppermint-breathed Dr. Mollins rebuilt
with the same tools he used on us, which then tooted,
coo-cooed, rang, ting-a-linged, buzzed, chimed, dinged
and clanged so clamorously you thought the year must have
turned, not just the hour. He seemed equally concerned
with his timepieces and our teeth. "Smile, you're on
Candid Camera," he'd say when we sat down. "Good,
very good. Soon you'll be perfect." He loved to document
our progress, roughly stuffing trays of claylike goo
into our mouths—"open wide, bite down, hold steady"—
that seeped through our teeth, not unpleasingly,
until they dried, when he wrenched them free
with some difficulty, leaving crumbly bits we spit and
rinsed out while he finished dating and numbering
the casts' upper teeth with a red felt pen and then
placed them in what he called his "Cabinet of Smiles,"
glass-fronted cases built nearly ceiling high
that surrounded us with his handiwork over the years.

Several decades later, when I ran into him in the lobby
of a Moscow hotel, he didn't know me at first.
"Smile," he said after an awkward while,
"you're on *Candid Camera*." Then, "Richard, how're

you and your brother Ken and pretty red-headed sister
Joanie and mom Gert?" With a fingernail he tapped
my overlapped two front teeth and said, somewhat sadly,
"You've regressed. Come in for a quick fix-up." Fat chance,
I thought. Saying, "Sorry, I'm late," I scurried away.
For by then my brother was dead and I wasn't perfect
in too many other ways to be worried that my teeth weren't
straight, including, at times, still being allergic to myself.

Rock Collection

I was a lonely kid
who collected rocks
and kept them hidden
in the bottom drawer
of an old desk
in a little-used room
off the kitchen,
lined up three across
like my toy soldiers,
though I enjoyed them
more, selecting favorites
each week that I would
place ahead of the rest
and think of as friends.
Some I chose for their
shape, like the round
flat ones I skipped across
the lake each summer
or the oval white piece of
dolomite that looked like
a spaceship on my favorite
TV show, *Captain Video*,
or the perfectly square
lump of coal I found
on the school grounds.
Though none were rare
they were beautiful to me:
quartz of all sorts—clear,
pink, rose, purple and blue—
limestone with clam and
snail shells still visible

or the spotted and striped
marble it could turn into,
glossy black obsidian,
petrified wood with striated
bark, greasy graphite I could
sharpen and write with,
amber with a bug inside,
cross-banded sandstone
with a fern-leaf fossil
imprinted on it, and talc
that powdered in my hand,
granite with embedded bits
of mica like tiny mirrors
that glinted brightly in light,
a pitted chunk of meteor
even older than the earth,
igneous lava rendered
in its red-hot center,
flint arrowheads I found
by the mouth of a riverbed
and polarized magnolite
that pointed north and south,
as well as clear and colored
crystals with multiple faces
showcased on velvet swatches.
One row was devoted to rocks
that turned into each other—
shale to slate to phyllite, schist
and gneiss—to me a magic
trick even though I knew
heat and pressure did it.
I also knew that diamonds
will scratch any other rock

and not be scratched back
but still borrowed my mom's
ring to prove it—luckily for me
it was true. And how I loved
the names I came across
in books: aragonite, wulfenite,
siderite, ulexite—like ancient
warriors from distant lands—or
tourmaline, sanidine, pegmatite,
oolite—the beautiful princesses
they rescued from certain death.
Little wonder I was so drawn to
rocks—they were everything
I wasn't: old and hard, fearless,
tested and nearly indestructible.
Even then I must have guessed
these friends would be unchanged
fifty years later when I was
clearing out my mother's house,
long lost but not forgotten.

Sweet Spots

I can't dance to save my ass, which refuses
to move in the music's groove. But once when
I was ten or eleven, playing in a Little League
game, I hit a ground-rule double
and can still recall, sixty years later, the exact
feel of the ball as it struck the fat part of the bat
and flew over the fence, and the sense
I had of being perfectly in tune with the
wider rhythm of the universe.

At sixteen, when I was captain of the high school
tennis team but far from the best player,
our coach skewed the seed—illegal to do—
by matching me up with the star of the league,
who went on to compete in the Junior Davis Cup.
I lost in record time but won one game with
three fast-paced, well-placed service aces and
they, not the loss, are imprinted on my body
and psyche to this day. I still watch as I
toss the ball high in the air in slow motion
and wait as it hesitates there quivering to
gather energy like the minute hand of a
bell tower clock before it strikes the hour,
while I twist my back and reach way up
to hit it squarely in the sweet spot of the racket.
I didn't even care when the next morning
a hateful rumor, totally untrue, flew around
school that my opponent took a taxi to the
court and told the driver to wait.

*

Years later I sat all day on a sandbar
in the sea, high on LSD, and swirled my arm,
seemingly detached from the rest of me,
through the water without being frightened
in the least. By late afternoon my hand
and a drifting crescent moon
began lifting tall waves with all their might.
I'll take these few moments of poetry
over the written kind, for the one rhymes only with
itself and the other with all of time and space.
They're much of what I know of Grace.

Learning to Shave

I wish I had a photo of my dad
and me staring into the bathroom
mirror wearing our underclothes
while he taught me how to shave.
We used so-called safety razors,
better than the old-fashioned straight
kind you sharpened with a whetstone
and folded back into itself like a
switchblade that didn't flick open,
but not nearly as foolproof as today's
disposable ones. We started out doing
a few practice runs using only the silvery
implement. After that he showed me
how to open its leaves by twisting the
bottom of the shaft, then thumbing out
a fresh blade from the ten-pack and
placing it on the track. "Preparation is all,"
he said, "as in painting a room," before
telling me to press a wet washcloth over
my face, hot as I could stand it, to soften
the stubble (though mine was more
downy than bristly at that stage) and
rub in a scoop of "soothing, medicated"
Noxema shaving cream from the
pretty deep-blue jar, which smelled like
eucalyptus trees and was sold on TV by
a sexy blonde lady who got me horny—
it didn't take much at that age—by purring
ever so slowly, "Take it *off*, take it *all* off."
Next, Dad showed me how to work up
a thick lather with a soft, badger-hair

brush (by far the best part). Only then
were you set to start, first shaving
the most exacting areas, below the sideburns
and on the upper lip, and then, using long,
smooth, downward strokes, the cheeks,
and shorter ones around and within
the rougher beard of the chin, grimacing
to tighten the skin, and upward thrusts
along the tough surface of the neck and
Adam's apple. Afterwards, you applied
a wet washcloth over your face once more,
this time cold, to close the pores. Then
you opened the razor's leaves to clean
the blade, and patted on greenish, mentholated,
sweet-smelling Mennen aftershave lotion,
which felt pleasantly prickly, except for
the half-dozen spots I had cut myself,
where the alcohol in it burned wincingly.
To staunch the blood my dad encouraged me
to apply a styptic stick, which hurt more.
Instead, I tore off bits of toilet paper
to sop up the flow and let it dry. As I
walked around the house, they stuck out like
tiny red-and-white handkerchiefs waving
surrender, but showed I was battle-tested,
with war wounds to prove it,
though clearly on the losing side.
The art of shaving was a lot like life itself,
Dad had implied—attention must be paid
lest painful mistakes be made that led,
to put it punningly, to losing face.

Now he took a look at me
and added, pretending sadness,
to tell the truth the art of shaving might be,
at the start, like death as well.
Though I suppose you could equally say
how good it is to begin each day by not
slitting your throat when you have
every opportunity.

II

A Conversation in Starbucks

Talking made their faces
twist like wrung-out rags.
Each word tortured through their lips
became a sagging strung-out moan as if
a child's finger pressed against an old LP,
their own private language that hurt to hear.
She tried to eat a bagel,
smearing cream cheese over her mouth.
He bent to sip coffee through a straw,
which still spilled over the rim.
It was hard to look at them.
They were sitting on motorized wheelchairs
powerful as horses (his had a skull and crossbones
sticker on it), wore sweat clothes
that failed to hide their crippled forms.
His sharp shoulder blades stuck out sideways
like masts on a storm-tossed ship.
Her "I love my cats" sock slipped
partly off an unshod foot.
They nodded oddly, in loose circles,
but the eyes of this married, middle-aged couple
pried steadily on each other.
When she made a joke his staccato
run of notes strangled in his throat.
Then they got set to go,
deftly do-si-do-ing to clear the table.
(Her wheelchair sticker read "Handicapable.")
There was a napkin on the floor
that his bony fingers hovered over
waiting to be empowered
to pluck like some magic flower.

After they left we all looked up
from our laptops and our books
as though coerced—but not quite—
to converse.

In Praise of Used Books

They're cheaper, of course,
so you can buy more.
They tell stories
beside the story—
rarely boring.
They pass from hand to hand
as wisdom can
and seldom come to rest.
They're guests
though often signed, dated
and addressed.
No worries about eating
while reading
and leaving coffee cup rings,
mustard stains
and the occasional
unidentifiable
sticky things.
(Who'll judge the smudge?)
There's the thrill of finding
a book you've looked
and looked for,
which more than offsets
broken bindings,
underlining that obscures
the text, bent pages
or other signs of aging.
Best of all
are the scrawled notes,
the fusillade of
exclamation points:

"Awkward!!!" "Misquote!!!"
"You joke!!!"
The circled spelling error
or mild question mark,
like a mother gently upbraiding
her misbehaving child.
Or the longer remarks
along several margins,
some stupid, some astute.
(What is white space for
if not to explicate more?)
You're joining a reading group
without needing
to get off your back
or provide the snacks.
And then there are
the betrayals, the heartbreaks:
"For Fred, like a brother"—
sold or traded for another.
"To Bette, my bunny rabbit"—
no more, alas, for you have it.

In Praise of Clichés

I laughed for a week the first time I heard,
at six, the phrase "It's raining cats and dogs,"
which still makes me smile when I see them
in my mind's eye tumbling pell-mell from the sky.
Long ago I lost an umbrella showing just that.
(Incidentally, why is it a dog's world, not a cat's?)

Writers are supposed to avoid clichés like the plague
but I say enjoy them to your heart's content,
a phrase Shakespeare invented as he did one I admit
to using without fully understanding it, "one fell
swoop," and others I agree with but in practice often
do the opposite, like "Brevity is the soul of wit."

Of course, being Shakespeare, he was also the first
to tell us why we should avoid his many gems:
"Tedious as a twice-told tale" goes doubly for them.
Phrases become clichés when they get stale by being
repeated ad nauseam. They're meant to surprise,
insist on being heard, find gold amidst the dross.

But I say clichés are as free as water, so why not
spend like there's no tomorrow and give them a spin.
A rug might be shedding cats and dogs, the day
pouring with all four paws, which also suggests
the way fog creeps in. If the best is the enemy of
the good, you should strive for the good enough.

Practice makes perfect but so does selection.
And isn't buying a cat in a bag less risky than
a pig in a poke, since you can always let the cat

out of the bag? But what could be finer than casting
pearls before swine? Thinking outside the box,
the bootless might say "pulled up by one's own socks."

If we're less confused than being at sixes and sevens
why not use at threes and fours? And shouldn't we
replace "dressed to kill" with "to impress DeMille"
or the even more obscure "dressed to the nines" with
"for headlines"? Enough! I'll stop on a dime, though
in inflationary times I'd prefer to say dollar bill.

A Note on the Type

The text of this book is set in Georgette,
a fine serif type designed to "kiss" the page
with an inky flow that's easy on the eye
and updated to reproduce better in a digital age.
The letters are seductive, even racy, in both cases—
elegant, confident, classic yet very contemporary,
and a touch aggressive with their finishing strokes.
The airy vowels a, e, o and u
float like soap bubbles about to pop
and moisten the i with a creamy dot on top.
This font has a friendly, open face with a
generously rounded body that's grounded
by shapely descenders on the p and y
tapering down to daintily shod feet.
But the lowercase g's are all belly
and breast like ancient goddesses.
The gorgeous Q uses its long tongue
to lingeringly caress the bottom of the u.
At the alphabet's center the O is so wide
open it practically cries out to be entered by
the stiff-angled M, semi-erect N, half-masted
H or the extended crossbars on the F and E.
The R's kick their stretched-out gams like
a chorus of showgirls at the Folies Bergère,
and the gentle swells on the b and d
mate well with their rigid straights.
The type has more than its share of ligatures
caught in the act, like the fl going at it
doggie-style, while the top row is equally
bold, with an amphora nearly genital
in its internal folds and an ampersand like a sheer

stocking tossed high before landing on the floor.
The spread-out V and tightly squeezed-together,
bent-legged W—well, quite enough said:
this font is not meant for a corporate report.

Writing: A Nightmare

I'm in a classroom taking
a timed writing test when my
pen runs out of ink and
the others refuse my request
for another. Panicked, I start
on a long slog through a
down-at-the-heels part of town—
empty Laundromats, used car
dealerships—until I come upon
a battered sign on a warehouse
door saying S ation ry Stor.
There a salesman with a mustache
that fails to hide his hairlip
goes to a far corner to show me
stacked pencils big as telephone
poles that come with a lumberjack
toting an ax to sharpen them.
"How much?" I ask him and he
says, "Three hundred forty-eight
thousand a six pack." "Dollars?"
"No," he jokes, "drachmas."
I shake my head and he points
to an elephant in the distance.
"He'll hold up to twelve gallons
of ink in his belly that he snorts
through his trunk. That one's a
sample but I can order you more."
When I let him know I'm not sure
it's affordable, he moves to a
"refillable" two-humped camel
and tells me, "This is a real deal—

it writes with what I like to
call its pen-is, is easy to grip
once it gets an erection and never
becomes parched *in medias res*
since it carries its own replacement
cartridge." When I look skeptical
he gestures to a row of skyscrapers.
"Let's get a pen and pencil set,"
he insists. "Thanks but no thanks,"
I resist, so he takes me to the
sale section, where there's a tank
with ink-filled snakes oozing
along the bottom. I choose one
and then run back to the class
but die on the way when
it bites me. I wake up thinking
he's sold me a poison pen.

On Balance

A circus performer tiptoes along a high bar juggling
flaming torches. The Leaning Tower of Pisa can
lean only so far before it will fall. A Calder
mobile's biomorphic forms jiggle in a
ghostly breeze, its meaning seen
mostly through spaces in be-
tween and shadows on the
walls. For balance is all
about what's left out
and what's not. A
perfect sentence
can perform
handstands
on a dot

.

III

Turning Seventy at a B&B on Clear Lake

Suppose for a moment I hadn't turned seventy that day
And the jagged hills didn't monitor my heart
Nor the grebes on the lake float their separate ways.

Lost friends and lovers flitted through my mind
Like the yellow-bellied warblers in the sedge.
Suppose for a moment I hadn't turned seventy that day.

I was reading a book about Caravaggio,
Short-lived sinner/saint of light and shadow
As the grebes on the lake fluttered their separate ways.

Then two of the birds paired off, their fluid necks
And pressed breasts forming a heart that soothed my own.
Suppose for a moment I hadn't turned seventy that day.

My wife and I held hands and stared in wonder
As the mates dove down for some grass to offer each other
While the rest of the grebes floated their separate ways.

They rose to their feet and skied off together so fast
And so far they left a wake of winking water.
Suppose for a moment I hadn't turned seventy that day
And seen the grebes on the lake dance away.

New Year's Eve at Seventy

In the early evening I undo the new
desk calendar and thumb its pages—
so clean and neat, so unforeseen—
before placing it on the cracked brown base
(but didn't I do this a month or two ago?)
and put the rubber-banded old one in a drawer,
then note the birthdays and anniversaries
of all those I want to call or light a candle for.
I doubt the flap-eared elephant in the room
will step on me before the year is out.
We leave to see a film—"Lincoln"—
before eating at a favorite restaurant—
Middle Eastern. We both have beet and feta
salads, then shish kebab for me, lamb stew
for Lucy. Home by ten to read—
a book on Titian for me, one on the earth's
condition for Lucy—slouching on kitty-cornered
couches, our feet, slippers off, meeting,
until we hear a lone horn outside blowing
raggedly, like a shofar on Yom Kippur.
We kiss and wish each other well,
doubting the flap-eared elephant in the room,
with its coronet of bells,
will step on us before the year is out.

Vanitas

1.

Those old Dutch masters, attuned to death
as much as life, saw all beauty sliding to ruin
and rarely showed a leaf without a wormhole,
a meal without mold, a plant without a wart,
highly prized tulips and apple cores or lemon
peels (signs of the bitterness of all existence)
whose edges weren't browned and wilted,
gilt-covered objects that weren't tarnished,
an unbent page or books that weren't aged.
When they said *nature morte* they meant it.
They found skeletons and skulls far more
telling than bodies and faces,
and even when they drew a floral bouquet
in all its glory, the moral was the same,
since everyone knew those they chose
grew in separate seasons, so in real life,
unlike still life, some would already be dead.
Beauty became truth in a latter day but for
these artists its essence portended its end.
They packed their pictures pell-mell
with signs of transience and evanescence:
bubbles, smoke, struck bells, snail shells, butterflies,
hourglasses showing the slow but ceaseless
flow of time and burned-out lampwicks.
Also symbols of fleeting earthly pleasures:
crystal vases, wine goblets (often overturned),
half-decayed Bibles opened to relevant quotes
and a kingdom's worth of jewelry—gold broaches,
emerald rings, strands of pearls, necklaces of
precious stones all laid out on velvet-covered tables.

Those grim Calvinists were determined to remind
humankind of our common lot, our fast-approaching
fate—diamonds may be forever but we're not.

2.

What, I wondered, wandering through museum halls,
would I put in such a painting on my wall?
Perhaps a small passport photo I keep in my desk
drawer to prove to myself I once had dark hair
to spare that I wore in a high pompadour.
And my old, rarely worn bar mitzvah watch,
solid gold, inscribed on the back "From Mother
and Dad"—neither alive—"June 19, 1955,"
which died decades ago and could not be revived,
since it needed a part from a defunct company
that also made a "perpetual-motion clock."
(When and where, I couldn't help thinking, will
my heart, still in perpetual motion, stop tick-tocking?)
And a frayed 32-inch cloth belt I keep in a cupboard
for nostalgia's sake with the pile of pants it held up.
I'd also include my fiftieth birthday party invitation,
a cartoon of me in every decade from ten to then,
like a Russian nesting doll, each a bit balder,
rounder and taller. Now I could add two more to it.
And my favorite bottle of wine, a sinfully expensive
Chassagne-Montrachet I ordered on a lark in Paris
one day, along with an almost as memorable dinner.
Or the car I just bought, a shiny red Infiniti,
of all names. Which of us will be the first to be traded in?
For color I might sprinkle in the mix of vitamins
and other pills I take that changes with every study
proving one or the other is a dud.
Then a dusty pile of books, part of the basementful

I thought I'd have time to read to get smarter.
Also the unabridged dictionary, *Webster's Third*,
Theresa left me before dying of ovarian cancer,
lovingly inscribed and kept open on an end table
to a word encircled by another friend of mine
because it is partly defined by a phrase in a book of his.
And even this poem, like all art a bid for immortality.
Will it be well-regarded a century from now?
Hardly. Ten years? One? A month? Not even,
I fear. Yet it somehow implants a tiny seed of hope—
after all, you're reading or hearing it now.

Dear Dad

It's hard to believe that you've been gone ten years
When Ralph Lauren and Cadillac and Sears
Write to you so often about their sales.
Don't they know that you are stiff as nails?

They're not alone in wishing you were here.
Offers come to fix whatever ailed
You, especially your eyes and teeth and ears,
To insure your life and health, to calm your fears.

The IRS says you are in arrears.
I tell them I can't make you reappear.
Though I've pleaded, wept and wailed, I've not prevailed.
I'm just a teller of tales, a sad sonneteer.

If you came back, it might not be much fun.
I send you all my love and remain
                    Your son.

Dinner With Mom

When I asked my father's business friend
On my twentieth birthday to recommend
A place in Paris Mom and I could go,
He said Panurge's Sheep "for ze food and show."

The name, I knew from reading Rabelais,
Meant to follow blindly, but we went anyway.
Displayed on walls and menus was risqué art
That featured enormous organs—not one a heart.

The sheep came over to sniff our private parts,
And everything we tasted from soup to tarts,
Like the engorged baguette over two round buns,
With anyone else would've been explicit *and* fun.

But the worst of all came from a room nearby:
Whispers of "*oui, mon chéri*" and mounting sighs.
We never mentioned it to one another.
Nor the similarity of mother and smother.

Remeeting Kenny

I don't believe in reincarnation but often have
imaginary remeetings with the dead.
The one with my brother is always a ride
he invited me to take with him on his favorite
four-cylinder Honda motorcycle around the
tree-lined streets near his home on Long Island
Sound when he was sick with cancer but a year
from dying at thirty-three. It happened in the spring—
the azalea bushes lining narrow roads abandoned
on weekdays were flowering, and heavily laden
oak and beech trees reached across to form
a green canopy that blocked the sky.
We couldn't talk with the wind in our ears—
just as well as we never had much to say,
although in those days, sharing the marijuana
joints he used to quell his nausea, the silence
felt more welcome. I leaned against him,
my arms tight around his worn brown leather
jacket, which seemed like such luxury
as we'd rarely been physically close since
we were infants in a bubble bath, diddling each
other's bean-sized penises or, later, getting
into trouble wrestling to an exhausted draw.
Or until I, older and heavier, sat on him
and pinned his thin arms to the floor.
(Forget about kissing, he was the only person
I ever tried to hug and missed.) He gave me
his helmet to wear—with incurable cancer,
why care? Even bald, he was handsomer
than I, his eyes somehow bluer and head
larger without his wavy red hair,

his pumped-up body not yet worn down
beyond repair. I always thought we were
opposites, but more likely our rivalry was so
intense we split ourselves in half, tennis for me,
baseball for him (how secretly proud I was
to watch him pitching in Little League!),
good grades, writing and humor for me,
popularity, mechanics and music for him.
We met on the backyard basketball court
in one-on-one games so fierce we came away
with scraped knees and bloody noses.
It's a pity, I thought when he died, that we
won't have the chance to find our hidden
halves. Then I got his letters sent to
friends and was surprised to see how funny
and literate he could be, if not with me.

For some reason, our remeetings all take place
in late fall under a Crayola-blue sky,
with a mango moon hovering overhead by dusk
and the breeze-blown husks of leaves sounding
as loud crunched under tires as the granola
I sometimes eat dry, or they scuttle ghostlike
on the ground around us, and the few left on
branches are all but dead, twittering on brittle
stems and venous red. When the wind
whips up, I lean harder into him,
my knees tight against his thighs as we sway
from side to side, and I feel sheltered also
by his expertise. The ride goes on even longer
this time, the loops he makes wider and wider.
We may never hug or kiss face to face, but this
is surely a kind of bliss. He would have been

sixty-nine today, and as is my habit,
I light a candle before his photo on the mantel
and wonder who we might have become
had brotherhood and death not sundered us.

Taste It

*For Liana Day-Williams, who
loved grilled cheese sandwiches*

Here's the way I make and taste
a grilled cheese sandwich these days:
first I take a single piece of rye bread
and spread a little light mayo over it
(I'm concerned about my waist),
followed by a thin slice of dill pickle
and thicker ones of cave-aged gruyere
and heirloom tomato, flesh-red and
glistening when in season. Then I
bake it on high in a toaster oven for
two or three minutes while I think of
Liana on a breathing machine in the
ICU and pretend this is my last
grilled cheese sandwich. When I
take it out I hesitate a bit before
closing my eyes and biting into it.

Five Recurrent Memories and a Metaphor

The one who came over a final time
before moving away so I could feel
the implants she got to surprise her fiancé.

The one who sent me, on a business trip,
a blown-up, life-sized
anatomically functional plastic lady.

The one who could rotate
each breast in a different direction
while juggling.

The one who insisted her wrists
be tied to bedposts on Sunday morning,
shortly before heading to mass.

The one who leaned out the car window,
her long hair sweeping the sunset,
her naked breasts showing the way
like Delacroix' *Liberté*.

The past is a broken-winged
seabird circling in mist.

Made in Bangladesh

Even on sale at twenty-nine ninety-five with another
forty percent off because it's a Wednesday
and free shipping for purchases over fifty dollars
to encourage me to order other stuff,
buying a polo shirt after the factory collapsed is
much more complicated than it used to be.
It's not simply that I already have so many
or that the new color, "string-bean green," looks
suspiciously like the "bell-pepper green" one I
recently bought (perhaps a little yellower if anything,
though it's hard to tell on a computer screen).
And it's not enough that the new polo has no corporate
logo to turn me into an ambulatory billboard
or that the shirt flap no longer drops lower in back,
which looks sloppy when I wear it outside my pants
to try to hide my belly fat, or that the brand-new
"Luxe" line is "baby-soft" to the touch,
much as I appreciate that, and woven entirely from
"fine long-staple Egyptian cotton," since any amount of
polyester in a mix tends to irritate my sensitive skin.
And I wish I could say my decision has been determined
solely by the murder of over eleven hundred workers,
most of them women, some not even in their teens,
in a building whose cracks they knew were growing while
they were sewing that day by an owner who made them
show up to get paid their ten-dollar weekly wage,
allowing me to buy the shirt for a little less, plus receive
enticing extras like a thank-you note saying I'd get
an even better price the next time I came online.

*

No, I cancelled the order because of a girl I met
in the back of a flatbed truck, riding north from Calcutta
in 1970 along the border of the soon-to-be hard-luck
country of Bangladesh, where the world's cheapest
clothes were yet to be made. She was a dark-skinned
beauty, seal-sleek, with a flexed bow's tensile strength,
soft brown iridescent eyes and promising smile,
who wore what I'd now describe as an avocado-green,
form-fitting sarong and halter that left a bit of bare midriff
in between, part of a troupe of young Bangladeshis
touring the tented camps where monsoon-soaked,
mud-bound refugees spent their endless days,
to instill in them, with songs and skits, some hope of
freedom and justice. I never knew her name but
over the years prayed her dreams didn't turn to dust.
If they did, she could easily be among the crushed.

The Art of Choosing

Paper covers rock:
For hours after the towers crumbled to dust
and the people burned to ash,
paper drifted down, patient as the sunlight
blocked from a flawless sky:
sell orders, love letters, insurance forms, blank
checks, date book reminders, resumes of the lucky
who didn't get the jobs and the unlucky who did.
It settled six inches thick on Trinity Cemetery
three blocks away, like an early snowfall
or white linen shroud.

Rock blunts scissors:
After the cell phone calls saying
"Tell the children I love them," a few
jumped or dove, piercing the bright protective
bubble we knew would burst some day
but hoped would end, as bubbles usually do,
with a soundless pop, a not unpleasant sense
of surprise and a slight sting in one eye.
Most raced the buildings down,
all slashing legs joined by
fulcrums of fear.

Scissors cut paper:
One week later an orange-overalled worker
used to clearing tickertape
after ballplayers and astronauts passed by
swept the fallen paper around the gravestones,
crying beneath his gas mask.
He fed it through the iron teeth of a garbage

truck, blind heedless beast that, roaring,
prowled the near-deserted streets,
passing a man saved by a fluke
that unsuspecting Tuesday morning.

He walked his son to his first day of school
through the lemon-colored early morning light.
The boy, a lunchbox-toting, tiny, tearful Yankee
in baseball cap and jacket, hugged the stony pillow
of his father's knees and then, as if sensing
the way was clear, dashed across the playground
where he would soon learn the art of choosing
using childhood games of chance
like paper, rock, scissors
or eenie meenie miney *mo*.

IV

Fetal Dreams

Perhaps their dreams are blurred abstractions,
a Pollock-like web of angry actions
turning, in deeper sleep, to a Rothkovian raft
of somber yellow to float on until they're
rescued by the riverbank.

Soon their dreams become semi-abstractions
like Miro's flying kites and paddling
paramecia, each with a few stray
hairs, an eye (never two) and something
that will soon become, I suppose, a nose.

Or maybe Freud was only half wrong
and infants long to be roped
inside their mothers' wombs
(fathers being too irrelevant to kill)
dressed in see-through silken robes,

rocking in a snug and food-filled world
of water exactly as salty as the tears
they shed after dreaming of the tadpoles,
newts and toads they once were.
Who knows why they cry.

Babies may have nightmares too,
including this recurrent one: it's a warm
and endless night, lapped by soothing
sounds, when suddenly all hell
breaks loose, an epic flood

followed by world-ending seizures
and howls to rouse the sleeping dead,
a headfirst plunge in a vise-like grip
through a dark tunnel
toward a blinding light.

Or could it be that at birth
babies dream their whole futures
in images that flash before their unseeing eyes?
A red tricycle, say, before a trellised
wall, or a chocolate cake with lights on top.

Doing the cha-cha with grandma, perhaps,
or a black cap flying toward a blue sky,
a white bouquet caught midair,
a lock of hair in a velour box,
a car, a boat, a colonnaded house,

a chaise longue on a lazy lawn,
a tiny casket lowered into earth,
or a snowy scene inside a globe of glass,
an ancient swaybacked collie on a couch,
a face glimpsed once and never lost.

Only the last one is familiar:
a hairless, shriveled being tethered
to food and water is seen dreaming
the very same dream in reverse.
The baby screams on waking to a life.

Ball Wall Ball

For Brandon, Age One

For the rubber ball
we used to call a
Pinky to bounce
back to my hand
when thrown
against a wall
was something
he had never seen
before. It left him
wide-eyed and
open-mouthed
with surprise and,
after, in a fit of
wild laughter.
"More," he gasped,
"more . . . more,"
still giggling so
hard he mostly
signaled for
nearly an hour,
when I stopped,
fearing his belly
would be sore.

The Discovery of Paper

For Devlin

He reaches for a single sheet
of the *Times*, all the news that's fit
to touch, beat, maul—or rhyme.
He shakes it, slaps it, twists it, hits it
with his fist, hears the rattle,
the rumble, the tumultuous battle
through tiny complicated ears,
pink and slightly translucent
like cyclamen petals in the light.
He watches it settle, tries to take in
the beastly thing through fearful eyes.
It smells like—what? Talcum
powder? His dribbling snot (he's nearly
eight months old and has a cold)?
His blankie's soiled silky edges?
His bottle's milky nipple? Pureed veggies?
He blows on it, sees it ripple, listens to
its quiet riot, bends it, folds it into place,
then back to its former space. He's pleased.
It's strong and supple like he is.
The corners of his mouth dimple into
quotation marks around unheard words.
He sneezes, then crumples up the sheet,
smooths it out, smiles, soothed.
When it suddenly tears, he reels back,
scared again. Paper's fragile, too,
like he is. He rips it once along
its length, then into strips and with all
his strength into tiny pieces. He tries
and tries to pull apart the tattered, twisted

bits. This matters. He pants, pillowing
his tongue against his two front teeth,
cheeks reddening. He can't.
The world's his toy, joyful and sad,
now scattered, destroyed.
He sweeps the mess into a pile,
then sends it flying apart.
He's riled but tired.
He sighs, twitches his runny nose.
His eyelids half close.
The future Phi Beta Kappa
(he's smart, if not Descartes)
leans back in his grandpa's lap,
ready for a nap.

Flow

He began
by tossing a
leaf into a puddle,
his raft, he said, and saw
it borne off by the breeze on
the water, then worked with the
feverish mind of a two-year-
old scientist needing to
know all there was
to know about
the physics
of flow.

Then he
chose some
twigs, his sea-
planes, he said, and
watched them go to and
fro in the swifter flow of a rivulet.
Next he picked up a stick, his
ship, and saw how it veered
this way and that in the
wider current of a
clear stream
nearby.

Next he
tossed in a
bigger stick, his
cargo ship, he said, and
noticed how it wiggled down
the center in its run, which he thought
was funny, so he giggled and then
threw in a section of a leafy
branch that was carried
away without ever
changing its
direction.

Finally
he struggled
with a large flat
stone, plopped it in with
all his might and watched it
sink, which made him stop and think.
Whoa, he said, it doesn't want to
float on top, so it couldn't be
a normal raft or boat or
cargo ship. It seems
more like my
submarine.

Peek-a-Boo

At two he likes to crawl
under people's sweaters
and stare out at the woven room
womb-warm in muffled expectancy
between dreaming and being awake
disappearing and being seen
wiggling his legs to draw you
to his secret place saying
"Peek-a-boo, I see you"
while he giggles and giggles.

I too like to sit
in cafes in midwinter
where the warmth of gathered bodies
mists the windows over
and people talk to one another
or stare at their phones
luring them to ring-a-ding
so they can shout "I'm here, I'm here"
as I peek at them while reading
needing to be found out.

Bugs

At four he likes dinosaurs, of course,
but what he really loves are insects
of all sorts, with or without wings,
tiny things he can crunch beneath
his feet or gently pat on their backs
as he pleases. He's learned about them
from books I've read to him
but more from exploring in the dirt
and grass of his yard. He knows they
like to hide in holes and expertly twigs
them out. "Look," he shouts, "a pincher,"
as he calls an earwig. "Don't come near it
or you might get bitten." Imagine animals
that feel with two hair-thin antennae,
view the world through dozens of eyes
and smell with six feet and you have
an idea of their surreal appeal to him.
He puts a kind of beetle—a black vine
weevil, he specifies—in a jar with holes
punched on top and feeds it a diet of dry
crumpled leaves. Sometimes he finds two
centipedes and tries to race them up opposite
sides of a cattail reed. Or he counts aloud
for me the seven black dots spread like
op art over the divided parts of a ladybug's
lipstick-red back, places it on his arm
and traces the slimy line it leaves behind.
He likes to watch spiders at work and test
the strength of their webs with sticks and
feathers he collects to put inside.
For him the emergence of bright-winged

butterflies from dull-colored, furry-crawly
things is a magic trick to beat all others,
but he seems to prefer the dark-brown
moths he finds half-hidden on tree bark.
(Perhaps blending in seems a surer means
of survival than screaming for attention,
although so far that's often worked for him.)
He approaches bees fearfully but won't go
anywhere near wasps. "They're poisonous,
you know." He follows worker ants as they
search for food and says they leave a scent
behind so others can find it too. He digs up
some earthworms, holds them by their tails
to show me how wriggly they become,
and tries hacking one in two, but it dies
instead of growing back the way he says
it should. "Worms aren't insects," he explains
with a hint of disdain. Then just when I feel
certain he's a budding entomologist—a bug
scientist, as I put it—he lets me know their
real appeal to him: "I'm the boss of them."

The Lost Turtle

I had a little turtle when I was five,
a round brown stiff-legged thing
with a yellow belly and a scalloped
black-ringed shell and hardly any ears
but a stretchy giraffe-like neck
who neither ran, nor swam, nor flew
and was easy to feel superior to.
I called it Sinbad for its wobbly seaman's gait
until, alas, I learned it was—hard to tell—
a girl and renamed her Myrtle, bell-shaped,
hand-sized Myrtle the Turtle, my first rhyme.
In her tall glass bowl filled with plants,
painted rocks and mounds of sand,
she scarcely moved at all but burrowed
underground, a helmeted soldier gone AWOL.
When I took her out to play and placed
obstacles in her way, she chose to go
around them, so easily did she tend to upend
into a shallow bowl kicking at the sky,
unable to roll over however much she tried.
Becoming stuck in your own hole
is such a silly way to die.
Then one day she disappeared, I don't
know how, but missed her very much
and looked for weeks under beds and rugs,
radiators, furniture, a loose floorboard,
behind books and even outdoors
where she had never been before.
How far from home can a little turtle roam
on thick legs heaving like galley oars?
Yet for years I dreamed of Myrtle making

her tortuous turtle way to—who knew?—
perhaps a zoo or out to sea where
she grew into a giant tortoise that might
live to be a hundred as some do,
mothering thousands of others on far-reaching
beaches and giving me, in time, an even
better rhyme—Myrtle the Fertile Turtle.
Or maybe she stayed close by to keep
an eye on me, as I, in my inconstant way,
still keep an eye out for her. If so
you could say she wasn't lost, just delayed.

V

A Blessing in Beige

The universe is really beige. Get used to it.
—John Noble Wilford, *The New York Times*

To Lucy

Some stars burn brighter as they age
Like maple leaves and apple trees flaming up from green.
Alas, the color of the universe is beige,

Not peach or pearl or the palest shade of sage,
Not turquoise, as they once thought—so serene.
Some stars burn brighter as they age.

The love that we have is harder to gauge
But it, too, burns brighter the later it seems.
Does it matter so much if the universe is beige?

As a poet breathes sound onto a silent page
Your love bathes my days in aquamarine.
Some stars burn brighter as they age.

Let them light up our lives as we leave this stage
And fill our hearts with their triumphant sheen.
Who cares if the color of the universe is beige?

A bird in flight outshines its silver cage.
If the sky's too bright the stars shine unseen.
May our stars burn brighter as we age.
Hurray, the color of the universe is beige!

Married Love

My wife always says she's
about to do something,
then she does it and after that
she tells me she's done it.
Does life lived according to
the strict rules of a dissertation
take all the fun away or triple
the communicational pleasure?

She looks at herself in mirrors
at every available opportunity,
when she's dressing, combing her
hair, doing her makeup (she uses
two) or even brushing, flossing
and rubber-picking her teeth,
which vastly decreases my chance
of getting a quick glance at myself.

About her clothes: she knows the price
of everything she wears and the precise
dates she bought them even in the distant past
and when she last wore them and with
what jewelry and other accessories.
I admire her memory but is it rude
for me to remind her to be on time
with half the same exactitude?

She's quite nice by day, a near Nazi
late at night when I long to read myself
to sleep. "For heaven's sakes," I say,
"it's my right!" and use the slight amount

of light three fireflies might make.
But she looks at me like I'm Jack the
Ripper holding a bloody knife,
which is almost as frightening a sight.

In a related item that comes up
before bed, we negotiate
how high to raise the windows.
Not a lot, she insists, a little more
I resist, so there's some fresh air to
breathe but not so much she seethes.
So heatedly is this repeated you'd think
we were discussing an international treaty.

She speaks more slowly than anyone
I know and never leaves a story incomplete,
its meaning implied or message not underlined.
If I try to speed her up she looks quite
surprised and I become contrite, apologizing
by saying what's true, that she's lightning
bright, and what's not: it's rather nice
to hear her every thought at least twice.

My wife is nothing if not precise.
She drinks eight glasses of white wine
a week, two on each of four nights,
never more but, bless her, never less.
Before driving she uses a breathalyzer
to test her blood alcohol level, so she can
relax without worrying about becoming
a dipsomaniac or ever getting arrested.

She plans ahead, to say the least,
buying raspberries, blackberries and
blueberries to top her breakfast cereal
along with two or three bananas
green as a summertime lawn.
In a few days when the berries are done
do you suppose the bananas have just
turned all yellow?. . . Hel-*lo*?

When eating she pre-cuts her meat into
tiny bites, inspects each lettuce leaf
for a speck of rot and washes her hands
like a surgeon as though a single germ
were a mortal sin that puts her life in peril.
This doesn't cause a fight but gives me
pause. "It's dinner!" I cry out in disbelief,
"not a sterile hospital procedure."

My wife likes to look tan and fit
and metabolize vitamin D
without shortening her life. So she
takes the sun by pretending to be
a chicken on a spit, rotating a quarter
turn every 7.5 minutes with a timer
by her side. Is there an earthly delight
she can't make into a task? Don't ask.

She keeps a typed to-do list of them
that takes up pages and pages,
neatly drawing a line through
each one when it's done.

But as the years go by and she ages
I can't help thinking about
the last. Will it be "The End"?
But then who'll cross it out?

Do You Love Me Even So?

Could there be
a better way to
begin the day
before the first taste
of milky coffee
completely bursts
the night's cocoon
than gazing on
my wife's face
while she awakens
in the early morning
shade-striped light
its still silken skin
after a dream-filled rest
and childlike smile
and glistening widely
spaced hazel eyes
questioning
do you love me
even so
as I do you?

The Girl With Cucumber Eyes

What will I be
thinking of
when death swoops
down noisily
from above
or creeps up
without a sound
to capture me
while I nap?
I'm quite sure
it won't be the
meaning of it all,
or the bright light
that's supposed to be
seen through a tunnel.
Not even, I fear,
the wife I love,
women I've been
enamored of
or the four grandkids
I adore. Nor the high
points of my life,
the errors I've made
and dearly paid for,
the places I've been,
houses I've lived in.
And what a surprise
it'd be if it's that
long-bearded old guy
in the sky wearing
a flowing white robe.

No, I'm fairly sure
it'll be something
rather obscure,
glimpsed briefly
or from far away,
accidental, wholly
unprovidential—
say, the girl with
cucumber eyes and
wet, taffy-colored,
tangled hair I once
met in a beauty
parlor, wearing a
celery-green smock,
her face, pasted white,
rendered smaller
down angled mirrors
until it disappeared
at the end.

Notes and Acknowledgments

Thanks to the editors of the following magazines and anthologies for publishing some of the poems in this collection: *Ambush Review*, *Blue Unicorn*, *California Quarterly*, *Cloudbank*, *Euphony*, *The Gathering*, *The Great American Poetry Show*, *Levure Litteraire*, *Marin Poetry Center Anthology*, *North Coast Literary Review*, *Painted Bride Quarterly* and *Tule Review*. The last nominated "Turning Seventy at a B&B on Clear Lake" for a Pushcart Prize. "New Year's Eve at Seventy" received first prize in the love category in the 2013 Ina Coolbrith Poetry Competition.

"The Discovery of Paper," "Peek-a-Boo," "Flow" and "Bugs" all come from observing my youngest grandchild and mini-muse, Devlin Pease, born June 25, 2010; "Ball Wall Ball" from his older cousin Brandon when he was around one.

"A Blessing in Beige" comes with a story of its own. When my wife, Lucille Lang Day, and I were planning to get married, we decided to write poems to each other as the centerpiece of the ceremony. We chose a common theme based on a recent newspaper article in *The New York Times* by John Noble Wilford explaining that, according to scientists, the color of the universe, if placed in a box and seen from a distance, was not turquoise, as they had once thought, but beige. We agreed to keep the poems a secret from each other until we read them at the wedding and were delighted to learn that we had both written villanelles (an old French form I came to like for its restricted rhyme scheme and the subtle changes in line repetitions) and used the same two sentences from the article as an epigraph: "The universe is really beige. Get used to it." It confirmed for us the inevitability of the marriage and seemed to augur well for its durability—so far, so very good. Lucy's wedding poem, "Color of the Universe," can be read in her collection *The Curvature of Blue* and on her website: http://lucillelangday.com. Both poems were printed on facing pages in the February 2004 issue of *Blue Unicorn*.

And lest anyone think that "Married Love" is anything but a good-humored complaint to balance the romanticism of the wedding poem, this may be the right place to say that my wife, a prize-winning poet and memoirist, read all of these poems many times and, in her gentle but persuasive manner, always made a pointed suggestion or two that improved them. Her enthusiasm for my writing has meant the world to me. Thank you, my love.

About the Author

Richard Michael Levine has written magazine articles for many national publications, including *Harper's, The Atlantic, Rolling Stone, New York, The New York Times Magazine* and *Esquire*, where he wrote a media column and was a contributing writer. He has been an editor or columnist at *Newsweek, Saturday Review* and *New Times*, received an Alicia Patterson Fellowship and has been a professor at the University of California at Berkeley Graduate School of Journalism. His bestselling book, *Bad Blood: A Family Murder in Marin County*, was published by Random House and New American Library and has been translated into several languages. A short story collection, *The Man Who Gave Away His Organs*, is available from Capra Press.

Also from Scarlet Tanager Books

Bone Strings by Anne Coray
poetry, 80 pages, $15.00

Wild One by Lucille Lang Day
poetry, 100 pages, $12.95

The "Fallen Western Star" Wars: A Debate About Literary California,
edited by Jack Foley
essays, 88 pages, $14.00

Catching the Bullet & Other Stories by Daniel Hawkes
fiction, 64 pages, $12.95

Luck by Marc Elihu Hofstadter
poetry, 104 pages, $16.00

Visions: Paintings Seen Through the Optic of Poetry
by Marc Elihu Hofstadter
poetry, 74 pages, $16.00

Embrace by Risa Kaparo
poetry, 70 pages, $14.00

crimes of the dreamer by Naomi Ruth Lowinsky
poetry, 82 pages, $16.00

red clay is talking by Naomi Ruth Lowinsky
poetry, 142 pages, $14.95

The Number Before Infinity by Zack Rogow
poetry, 72 pages, $16.00

Call Home by Judy Wells
poetry, 92 pages, $15.00

Everything Irish by Judy Wells
poetry, 112 pages, $12.95

*Turning a Train of Thought Upside Down: An Anthology
of Women's Poetry,* edited by Andrena Zawinski
poetry, 100 pages, $18.00

www.ingramcontent.com/pod-product-compliance
Lightning Source LLC
Chambersburg PA
CBHW022202080426
42734CB00006B/554